My Favorite Tyrants

THE BRITTINGHAM PRIZE IN POETRY

# My
# Favorite
# Tyrants

Joanne Diaz

THE UNIVERSITY OF WISCONSIN PRESS

The University of Wisconsin Press
1930 Monroe Street, 3rd Floor
Madison, Wisconsin 53711-2059
uwpress.wisc.edu

3 Henrietta Street
London WC2E 8LU, England
eurospanbookstore.com

Printed in the United States of America

Library of Congress Cataloging-in-Publication Data

Diaz, Joanne, author.
  [Poems. Selections]
  My favorite tyrants / Joanne Diaz.
      pages cm. — (The Brittingham prize in poetry)
  ISBN 978-0-299-29784-8 (pbk. : alk. paper)
  ISBN 978-0-299-29783-1 (e-book)
  I. Title.
  II. Series: Brittingham prize in poetry (Series).
PS3604.I18A6    2014
811'.6—dc23
                              2013027989

# CONTENTS

3

## Metastasis

# Acknowledgments

Poems in this collection have appeared in the following publications and web pages:

*AGNI*: "A la Turka"

*American Poetry Review*: "Larry David on Corregidor," "Pyrrhic"

*Cerise Press*: "What My Father Eats"

*Cumberland River Review*: "Erasure"

*DIAGRAM*: "Thank You, Brian Williams"

*Memorius*: "Little Terror"

NEA Writers Corner web page: "Metastasis, Boracay"

*Quercus Review*: "Cuba Libre"

*Southern Review*: "Adamantine," "Barbershop," "Emerson in Mourning," "Purgatory Blues"

*Spoon River Poetry Review*: "77 Porter Street," "The anatomy of my melancholy,"
    "Demeter's Last Stand," "Duende," "On the Meeting of Larry David and Antonin
    Artaud," "Take Up and Read," "Uncle Ming Pinched Me"

*Third Coast*: "Pride and Prejudice"


Special thanks to my most thoughtful readers: Katy Didden, Ann Hudson,
Jane Lin, Deborah Ryel, Cassie Sparkman, Grace Talusan, Angela Narciso Torres,
and Laura Van Prooyen.

# 1

## THE
## PERIMETER
## OF PLEASURE

# LARRY DAVID ON CORREGIDOR

The last thing the island of Corregidor needs is my correction,
　　but when I climb the staircase of the lighthouse and see the ruins
of what were tennis courts built by Filipinos for American officers,

　　the scent of sampaguita flowers wafting around and above
where the net once drooped, I have to ask: *The courts were built by Filipinos*
　　*who served in the front lines, but they could not play on them,*

*not go near them?* And though I know the tour guide's answer
　　before she says a word, I cannot stop myself.
Who ordered the tennis balls? Who restrung the rackets?

　　Who swept away the puddles early mornings
during rainy season? In the distance, we can see the path
　　of the Bataan Death March where thousands died, malarial,

diarrheal, bloodied by brutal force in a procession that violated
　　every convention and rule of decency; and to the right,
the haunted Malinta Tunnel, where the ghosts of soldiers

　　who typed and radioed and telegraphed underground for months
are shooed away by the "sight and sound" show three times each day.
　　I would have done better to ask about the separate barracks,

the single row in the back of the island's movie theater,
　　the ward in the old part of the hospital—but still I'm preoccupied
with the tennis courts, and in the moment that the tour guide stares

　　at my fourth question, I realize that I'm behaving like Larry David,
great dissenter in all things mundane, fighter for no one and yet
　　resister to everything beyond his own skin, symbol for all

that refuses to be corrected, straightened out, made right. And though
　　I am embarrassed by the Puerto Rican Day parade episode
and the Chinese take-out guy from the *Seinfeld* years, and though Monena

the black prostitute in season 4 of *Curb* leaves me feeling ashamed
of a writer who would create such a sassy, large-bosomed role, still
    I am Larry David on this most absurd of strategic islands. I care less

about MacArthur's selfish, barrel-chested promise of "I shall return"
    or the godlike, seven-foot bronze statue of him where the tourist trolley
stops for photographs. I care even less about President Quezon's

    fatal, hacking cough, brought to life on the recording during the "sight and sound"
so that we can relive his tubercular demise; or the rubble of bones
    that litter the regrown forest and circle the posts of the broken pier.

All I want to know is this: in those lean years before the Second World War,
    who caught the stray balls that were shot way over the fence?
Who painted the lines after the sun burned them all to dust?

# LITTLE TERROR

To his mother he was *Little Soso*; to the people
in his impoverished village, *Dhugashvili*,

and even if some linguists claim that his patronymic
means *son of garbage*, even if one of his arms

was slightly longer than the other, for one year
when he worked at the observatory in Tbilisi,

he was handsome, and his mother adored him,
choler and all. She knew that when he lay at night

beneath the Georgian stars, his pockmarks
vanished, and his arms seemed the same length.

These nights at the observatory came many years
before he would forsake his own son rotting

in a German prison, before his wife would kill herself
from shame and neglect, long before

he allowed millions of Russians to starve. He was still
*Soso*, astonished by the dignity of stars, the names of which

owned nothing, claimed nothing, but pointed toward
a sweet desire: *loincloth, solitary ones, little belly, wonderful.*

## Pyrrhic

Art can make war look wrong, but most of the time
it doesn't. Consider this terracotta jar, once filled
with olive oil to anoint the dead, now a souvenir
of fire, clay, and spittle standing in the back
of the Ancient Wing. Look closer: some dancers
are clothed in robes, others are naked, and all
wear helmets while the musician plays a double flute
and taps his toe. First, they join hands, then the delicate,
ceremonious footwork begins. The collective line
leans backward, shoulders shake slowly, then faster,
then they agitate their feet, which glide in front
and to the side until—listen to it—the flute's trill
is a frenetic scream, a hot coal that burns
beneath them until the enemy is nearly visible
in the dirt. The kicks get harder, then
they're on their knees in a circle, and then up again,
stronger, ready to throttle the man who must have
wronged them. The men are young and this is a song
of war, a military drill meant to ruin the worst tyrant
ever known to man. For the pyrrhic to work,
it has to thrill every bone. It has to feel like sex
or food or applause until they're numb to cowardice.
The driving beat has to make the enterprise
seem clean—no blood on the shield, no innards
on the pike, no burning flesh to smell like cooked meat,
no orphans, no widows, no crime. Art can make war
look wrong, but most of the time it blurs bright, blossoms
red, and burns forever at the dancer's feet.

# Duende

At a pre-concert talk for a new opera inspired by Lorca's life,
the conductor asks the composer, *What part does duende*
*play in your work?* And the man sitting beside me leans over

to ask, *What is duende?* I whisper, *a fierce magic, a melancholy spirit,*
believing that he will follow the social contract we have agreed upon
by sitting quietly in his chair. Instead, he pauses, then leans in

to joke, *Yesterday I thought I had duende, but it was gas.*
Perhaps *duende* burrows like a rare seed in the red soil
of Andalusia, only to rise through the mists of Galicia

until everyone in Spain swoons under its spell. But that's
not right: I know the seed grows here, too, because
my childhood in America had *duende* in spades, well before

I knew its name. Do not misinterpret this: I have no sad stories
about my labors over a lathe or hard years of factory work
in the city. My parents lived that life so that mine

would be so easy as to be nearly nonexistent. But every easy life
is crowded with the ghosts of those who suffered for it. I spent
most days in sympathy for those ghosts, longing

for something I had never lost, learning the look and sigh
and sway from *mediterraneos* like Mrs. Lobos, kind neighbor
who, like all the women of my youth, had giant eyes and breasts

to match. One summer, she hired me to assist her in secretary work
at the middle school, and though I can't imagine now
what I must have done to fill those hours, I do remember

the afternoon that Mrs. Lobos brought her face to her hands
and wept, wordlessly, for minutes. By this point in my youth
it came as no surprise that an adult, familiar or strange,

would weep before me. In films, it was Anna Magnani,
pulling at her hair as she ran through the streets of Rome;
at parties it was the women at the table, raging against the woes

of motherhood. But this was no party: this
was fluorescence in every corridor, Lysol in the toilet stalls,
and telephones with red flaring buttons. In her sorrow

Mrs. Lobos did not rant or rage, blame or curse.
She merely whispered, *Mr. Lobos has left me. I guess
he got tired of being married.* Beyond us, the sun-parched fields

led to the track that no one used in summer, and to the shadows
of the school, where young men rested after mowing acres
of stiff crab grass. Eventually, Mr. Lobos came back

without fanfare, and Mrs. Lobos never spoke of it again,
but for months after that day, when I rode by their house
on my bicycle, I would wonder, what wolves are they?

What secret sorrow do they harbor? I knew then
that American *duende* isn't the grief of a man's leaving,
but the feeling that comes when he returns.

## Motor City

In Detroit, there are so few cars on the streets
that I begin to imagine the absence
as a loss of blood in the veins of a dying man.
This afternoon we drive down historic Woodward Boulevard,
the spine that links the fragile bones of the city,
to the now-abandoned Tigers Stadium,
where Jay stops to take photos of the ruins that seduce him.
As I wait in the Toyota, I hear what must be crows
troubling the upper rafters, and I picture Vulcan
living there, sledging at a makeshift forge,
his loincloth sweat-soaked, his long back rippled
with muscles. Vulcan, great god of blacksmiths
and metallurgy, ugly and misshapen at birth,
an ugliness worsened by the arsenic that slowly poisoned
all the workers of the Bronze Age; Vulcan, more bound
to the elements of this earth than any other god.
A short mile away from here, a game is about to begin
in the new stadium. Bacchus feasts on hot dogs
from the Tiger Den Lounge; Jove settles into his luxury box seat
to slurp cold beer from a plastic commemorative cup;
and Venus and Mars have sex in their very own
baseball-shaped cab on the Ferris wheel. If he were mortal,
Vulcan would have died of shame many times by now,
but he cannot die, cannot look away. From his fossil
of white and turquoise tin, he can, if he squints, see
the rocking of their cab, but Vulcan is never idle.
He is already hard at work on a metal net, which,
when thrown upon his wife and her lover, will capture them
in their incriminating embrace. Done with ruins now,
Jay walks back to the Toyota and we spin out
of the empty parking lot. Behind us, Vulcan
forges the final link. He casts the net across the city,
over the lovers, and over the giant limestone tigers
that rage defiantly at each entrance of the stadium. How easy
for love to go so wrong. How wide the holes in the net.

Lucretius scorned those who believed that fire
is the basis of everything, but if Lucretius had lived

in our apartment, even he would have conceded
that we thrived at the center of all things fire.

Once, the plastic pitcher wed itself
to the stovetop's orange coil; at parties,

your long cigarettes smoldered in the ashtray
near Hilda's side of the patio, and we watched,

bemused, as she poked the tray away with a hockey stick;
and on a separate occasion, a fire mysteriously started

in the oven and I came home to find you huddling outside
with other neighbors including Jacinta Diaz, her name

and life nearly mine except for her subscriptions
to pornographic magazines wrapped in brown paper.

Even Jacinta trembled beside you in that night's wintry haze
as the firemen poked at the cinders that fell into the dimples

of our orange linoleum. Weeks later, the ruined fire
from our kitchen was reincarnated in the triple-decker

on the corner, built by laborers over one hundred years ago.
By six o'clock one morning that house was sticks of flame,

charred vinyl siding, the smoke from kitchen grease
saturating the curtains. The firemen seemed to recognize us

as we leaned over our patio railing's rungs, still warm in our pajamas
as the now-homeless strangers—weepy, confused, tired,

ill-clothed—watched the March snow melt a wet halo
around their house, the smoke mixing with fog,

enlarging it, altering its composition. When it was time to leave
77 Porter Street for our new lives, we were last-minute

in our packing, even though we had known and planned
for months. My last glimpse was in daylight: a blue bottle

broken in the corner, dust balls drifting like tumbleweeds
through the living room, a shadow where the old television

once glowed. Grace, one day I will be as old as stone, but
even then I will never separate that heap of steel and glass

and dust, its wooden floors, its cement patio with the single red bulb,
from you. When, as bodies do, ours break down to mere traces

of life; when our experience includes no more than a circle two feet
from ourselves; when our struggle to wake each day is the perimeter

of our pleasure, will you remember those days of fire,
when we burned to touch and be touched by all things?

begins with his body, standing as it did
twenty years ago in the lamplight that cast a circle
on the stairs, his eyes looking up, one foot
on the first carpeted step, the other slightly turned
as if about to leave. Or, it begins like this:
his long stretch after a day's work
at the auto body repair shop, hands creased with oil
from hubcaps, alternators, fan belts, screws
of every size, even his thumb and index finger
pressed into muscle. His hands on the gears
of his bicycle, the hairs on his legs brushing against
the spokes, the gentle cleaning and fixing and resting
on the seat, waiting for his provocations to take effect.
No line divides his body from the etching
on the dashboard of his Chevy Nova that read
*NFC* for *No Fat Chicks*; no boundary separates
the grooves in the vinyl seat from the body itself.
Whatever his body touched touches all things now.
His body does not stop its weaving; it is always
just released from its weight-lifting belt as he leans
against the counter, the marks of his mother's Spanish
rubbing against his English. He is wings of hair
on the sides and waves of longer hair in the back,
all of which could take flight as tufts of grass
as he reclines on the front lawn. He is the small pane
of glass on the door that, if you look closely,
reveals him leaning in over the book, waiting
for the tutee to respond. He is the concrete monolith
that houses the lab at UMass Lowell, the table
in the lab, the questions, the circle around the table
to get to the instruments. He is in the petals and leaves
of every specimen; the inertia behind the force
that props the blossoms into bloom. His body is a shell
for the gentian before it is gentian, before language,

before blossom, before decline, before the bee
that hovers and borrows, before the rain is absorbed
without reverberation. He is the spools of dust
that lace the leaves, and he is the rows of seeds
in too-near sun, their proximity to both dark
and bright in the imprint of the past. Even now,
in this digital photo from the present, even with
the surprise of a tired face and graying hair,
even here in this utterly common pose with a wife
in front of a castle, his image is the scaffolding for all
melancholy. Watch as the small photo enlarges, its pixels
wide and diffuse, until all is a blur of golden squares.

## Dog Whisperer

Hail Cesar Millan, great whisperer of the descendants of Cerberus!
From Ft. Myers to Anaheim we sing your praises!
For you can stop Nunu the demon Chihuahua from bearing his tiny teeth

at every stranger. For you can train Emily the pit bull to walk
beside another of her species as if she were a friendly suburbanite
and not a member of a bloodthirsty breed. For you can transform

Gavin, a K-9 who served dutifully in Iraq, from shell-shocked war veteran
to healthy Labrador who receives the occasional acupuncture treatment.
For you can do all of this in the span of a twenty-seven-minute episode

bracketed by previews for other shows of savagery and might.
But not even you, great Cesar, could tame the woman who loved her dog
more than her own son. You gave the mother two options:

to control her dog or allow her son to be bitten, abused, and injured.
As the mother considered her options, the dog sneered
at the small boy, channeling the spirits of the clay guard dogs

that the most affluent ancient Assyrians buried beneath their homes.
Ten clay dogs, two painted in each of five colors and inscribed
with names like "Don't think, bite!" "Biter of this foe!" and "Loud in his bark."

The mother considered Cesar's ultimatum and declared, *I will never
abandon my dog*, as her son cowered in the corner. Cesar, even you,
mighty emperor of the dog behavior world, could not provide

an antidote for that. The purpose of those clay figurines was to guard
against the evil spirits outside the house. But what about the spirits *inside*,
infected, wild beyond recognition, adept at eating their young.

## Queen Bee

Whenever my mother walked into a restaurant,
        she'd check every utensil for a smudge
and if she found one, even if all four of us
        had squeezed into the booth, she'd snap

her fingers. Time to leave. But even if
        she saw clean forks and a tabletop free
of butter pats and ketchup stains,
        there were other tests. When the waitress

approached our table, my mother would insist
        on calling her by name throughout
the meal, sometimes at a reasonable volume,
        sometimes loudly if Doris or Pat

or Sue were rushing past with a tray
        of heavy plates. And then, the final test:
the bill, which, even if my father was the one
        carrying the cash, had to be examined

by my mother as if it were a strike against her
        that required a strike back.
She was, as Henry James would say,
        one of the people on whom nothing was lost.

In this world there is a lot of losing
        to take, but she had to take so little:
she had left the city for a new house, saved
        for a good retirement, lived a life nearly free of violence,

and she had, through these things,
        become white in the America
that would have counted her people as a separate,
        squalid race only a few decades before her birth.

At her wake, Art Trepaney took me aside
        and said, *Joanne, you were your mother's pride*
*and joy, but she made you work for it.* That summer
        after her wake, I spent most mornings

hiding by a juice machine in an industrial kitchen,
        feeling that nausea from every restaurant
of my youth. One morning, when I asked
        one of the regulars, *Would you like some juice?*

she took a moment to look at my nametag,
        nodded, and said, *Joanne,* then examined
the fingerprints on her amber-colored glass
        as if she were a baroness in a Merchant Ivory film,

a high-minded lady only used to the highest
        standards of service from family and wait staff alike,
and though I didn't know this woman, I could see
        that for her, love was a test that no one could pass.

# Archaeology

Each time I have read Job's complaint, I have thought,
What's worse? The misery of losing one's children
and wealth, the humiliation of a wife's contemptuous curse,
the pain of unsightly boils and ash on the skin,
the doubt of a handful of alleged friends who say,
*Surely, you must have done something to deserve this,*
or a visit from a God who reminds you that you are abject,
a mite on the border of subjectivity, utterly powerless
in his midst, precisely because he created you that way?
Impossible to know Job's misery; impossible to fathom
his silence at the end of that book, which, in the end,
may be even more compelling than his lament. In that silence,
I can imagine him understanding a thousand varieties
of misery in the world, especially those
that have become only more creative over time.
What might Job have thought of the many doctors who,
when commanded by Franco's men, took thousands
of newborn babies from their mothers as they trembled
on the delivery table. It took only a few moments
for the doctor to leave the room and then return
with a somber look, a simple story of loss
and God's plan, a death certificate typed
on a typewriter that skipped a little each time
the typist used the "A," and a promise
that a tiny wooden coffin would offer the baby shelter
as its body and spirit endured the inevitability of Purgatory;
and then, while that story was told, there would be another
unfolding, a miracle play of sorts, in which the gravedigger
would push his hoe into the ground behind the hospital
then bury the empty coffin, and the typist who composed
the death certificate would type a birth certificate as well,
but this time for a different name, and no parents,
so that the baby who never died would live as a phantom

in a Spanish orphanage. Such creative work
to ensure that Franco's babies would not
lean to the Left, not tell the secrets of the fallen,
not ever try to win the Republic back. For Franco, the world
did not contain enough mystery, enough unsolvable crimes.
How much more interesting to have a nation of orphans
grow to adulthood, every day looking into the eyes of every mother
on every park bench, every last one a helix full of dissidence
living up to the Latin archaeology of that word, *dissedere*,
to sit apart, to be foreign to one another, to never know
the other's truest name.

## A LA TURKA

Tonight is belly dancing night, and so we revel in the abundance
of a young, loose belly, barely concealed by a black veil,
shimmering beside a boy who, at six or seven,
is a most earnest dancer, satisfied at first to wave his arms
from his chair, then midway through the first song,
to leave his family at the table and slink swivel-hipped
toward the belly dancer. Everyone in the restaurant
laughs approvingly, the sound quickly absorbed
by the tapestries on the walls, the Oriental rugs on the floors,
the chairs' upholstery, and the napkins on our laps.
And why not have some fun? It's a birthday for us,
an anniversary for them, or a new job, or a baby,
the eggplant is succulent and bitter, the Sultan Special
quite savory, and all is so good as we sip our yogurt drinks
that it seems in poor taste to mention the crudely painted portrait
of Kemal Atatürk on the wall, flanked by two yellow scimitars,
directly above Jay's head. For a moment I have to wonder
whether to think of Atatürk as the father of modern-day Turkey,
or a war criminal, or both, which seems unfortunate
in such a happy place, and so well-carpeted. But maybe
a portrait of the man who with the stroke of a sword
joined in the killing of thousands of Armenians
and with the stroke of a pen ordered a new last name
for every Turkish subject isn't so bad. At least the Turks
had the decency to bury his body; just today I read an article
about the remains of Vladimir Lenin, how the Russians
don't know whether to leave his embalmed corpse on display
or finally bury it beside his mother's remains, even if
he wasn't Christian, his body ravaged by syphilis. But whether
it's because the glass case isn't airtight or because
he has special fungal powers, he's sprouted more mold
over the years than the Ussuriysky Forest. And who
has to clean that up? Who has to open the case after
viewing hours, dip the body in glycerol, and retouch the spots

where his lips have cracked? Don't get me wrong—
I have my favorite tyrants. When the boots are shiny
and the hair neatly combed, it means that a group of people,
however misguided, lusty, or downright hateful,
have collectively agreed to make a fuss, be modern, and,
if not handsome, at least clean. And that cleanliness
has always counted for a lot in a world where its promise is a kind
of food. I know that it's Jay's birthday, but it's hard to ignore
Atatürk's acrylic glare, especially when the meal has been so fine
and there's still the question of baklava or pudding or tea.
This painting will not decompose like skin or require constant bathing.
It's astonishing, that face, like a clean machine made of sadness.

# Thank You, Brian Williams

My gratitude begins during your coverage of the Winter Olympics
when, during the opening ceremony, you announce sotto voce
that Italy has the third largest number of troops on the ground

in the wars in Iraq and Afghanistan. Thank you, Brian Williams,
for this brief lesson in military might. I was so preoccupied
with my admiration of those smart berets worn by every athlete

regardless of nation or creed, so transfixed by Pavarotti's
donut-like comportment under his billowing tent-of-a-cape,
so haunted by Venetian puppets that will linger in my dreams

that I had forgotten Italy's willing collaboration.
Thank you, Italy! And dear citizens of Turin!
Such might deserves acknowledgment, even if it's only

a bronze-level effort. Italy, you know your talents—your noodles,
your shroud, your art, your status as charming tourist destination.
Even better, you have the decency to change your government

when your leaders try to throw your country down the crapper,
and several months from now, you will be honest enough
to withdraw your forces from those doomed and bloodied

desert nations. But we Americans have talents too. We are still
number one, we love values, and we have you, Brian Williams.
And your wise and folksy insights do not stop at Turin.

You were right to encourage us to see *United 93*, a very important,
highly dignified, and supremely patriotic film! It is nothing
if not a tribute to good taste and *a badly needed reminder for some*

*that we are a nation at war because of what happened in New York*
*and Washington and, in this case, in a field in Pennsylvania.*
I'm not sure which war you mean, or who the *some* are

that need reminding, or who you think brought those planes down,
but no matter. Your rhetoric stirs me; your eyebrows
are at the helm. When I hope for certainty you provide it:

when you ask the president what he read last summer,
I am relieved to hear Camus's *The Stranger* and three "Shakespeares,"
glad that for once he might have given pause over the death

of one Arab, albeit a fictional one on a beach, and that perhaps,
when reading those three Shakespeares, he thought,
if briefly, of *the purple testament of bleeding war.*

# 2

ELEGY

ERASURE

The news of the death
               broke down the barriers       of endurance.

        I lacked the
patience        to represent    that degree of grief:
                              wretched mother
                              at last transformed into a rock.

        The impact,
               the hot alarm        of the soul—
my senses
               subtle fire,
               my ears,
                       both eyes
the body weighed down
        by the surprise—

        such an excess
                of human frailty.

## Barbershop

To get there, drive past Hajjar Elementary School,
named after the child of Lebanese immigrants
who lived here his whole life and died as the much-loved war hero
and town physician. Coast past the ditch where the now-filled
Middlesex Canal once traversed the town lines of Billerica,
Burlington, Winchester, Cambridge, and Boston, transporting
raw cotton in one direction and colorful textiles
in the other. Take a left at the corner of Call and Pollard,
there at the house of Asa Pollard, the first man to give his life
in the Battle of Bunker Hill, twenty miles southeast of here.
Follow the necklace of shabby little ranches on Pollard
until you get to the town center, then drive around the rotary,
built around the tree beneath which George Washington
allegedly sat—is there any town in the former colonies
that doesn't have such a tree?—and keep turning
past the old town hall, which is the new library, then
the old library, which is now the senior center
where she got her flu shot the day before, then past
Sweeney's funeral home where she is now, in the basement,
beneath the hands of the mortician who injects her veins
with the formaldehyde that will preserve her until the next day,
when the hearse will drive her coffin to a plot that is being dug,
past Taylor Florist, where they will charge four hundred dollars
for a spray of lavender wrapped with cheap ribbons that say
*Mother* and *Wife*, to Jim's, where you can see my father
getting his first barbershop haircut in forty-eight years.
The sideburns, already, are not to his liking, and the razor's edge
feels a size off from her Oster home barbershop razor,
and the plastic sheet that covers him now is so uncomfortable
compared with the flowered bed sheet that she used, stained
purple-brown as it was from years of her own home coloring treatments.
If you listen, you'll hear him tell the barber that he hasn't been
to a barbershop since 1961, but now that she is gone, he guesses
that this is what he'll have to do. In these first days, he's relieved
to be with strangers. With them it is almost easy to say,
*My wife has died* in this, his new language.

## Purgatory Blues

The word comes from *purgare*:
to make clean, to purify.
I say the word comes from *purgare*:
to make clean, to purify.
I thought that would impress you.
You searched for word roots while I died.

I left before my last rites:
no forgiveness for my soul.
No time to shrive with last rites,
no repose for my soul.
When the atheroma clogged my blood flow,
sin just left me all alone.

It's just as well. I would've told the priest
that the Church is full of shit.
I would have told that lackey
that his Church is full of shit.
If he had raised his hands to bless me,
I would've roused myself and spit.

When you go to St. Gertrude's,
don't you kneel and pray for me.
When you go to St. Gertrude's,
don't you weep and pray for me.
The only thing that I demand
is your apology.

Until you say you're sorry,
this fire will singe my hair and skin.
Until I know you're sorry,
this fire will burn my hair and skin.
This in-between may be for my wrongs,
but you are also steeped in sin.

You ignored all of my wishes
though I'd rehearsed them one by one.
You didn't read my donor card
or burn my ashes in an urn.
Just like when I was living,
you shut me down when I was gone.

You buried my body in haste
as if I had some strange disease.
Buried without a eulogy!
I felt like some strange disease.
Couldn't hit the plot soon enough
in that cold October breeze.

Medieval folks here tell me
there's such a thing as dying well.
I know the *ars moriendi*:
it's the art of dying well.
One day I'll get to leave here,
but right now it feels like hell.

## ADAMANTINE

In hushed tones, the funeral director discusses
the options—cremation and pouring

into a tiny pot, like a lusty ancient Roman;
wake, then cremation, then pot,

like an ambivalent Protestant; or wake
and traditional burial, like an adamant

Catholic—and soon he is referring to
the cremains of my mother. *Cremains.*

Does a trademark symbol follow that word?
Does the funeral director get a commission

every time he uses it without irony?
Did he adopt it after a funeral directors' conference

where they gave him a complimentary vinyl bag,
name-tag lanyard, breakfast vouchers,

brochures on the newest eco-friendly caskets,
and pamphlets from the Cremation Association

of North America, whose statistics confirm
that cremation is indeed a burgeoning market

growing every year by at least 1.5 percent?
While the director insists on saying *cremains*

at least four more times, my poor father
holds his head in his hands and wishes

he had been the first to go. But if death
had come for my father first, and if she

were the one who had a checklist
for everything that needed doing,

even she would have smirked at *cremains*
and said, *My husband's dead and you're making up*

*words, and then you're gonna charge me*
*the same whether he's in a box or in a pot?*

In the end, my father will ask for the only rites
he and his friends have ever known: the wake,

the burial, the stone above her head, the purchase
of an empty plot beside hers, so that when

he visits her grave, which he will do,
he can imagine her in one piece

with the strident voice he heard
for over fifty years. *If I get cancer or Alzheimer's*

*or Lou Gehrig's disease, just buy a gun and shoot me,*
she used to say casually, as if illness and death

were many years away. *And then, have me cremated*
*so that I don't have to lie there like a goddamned fool.*

# The Nurse

When she looked at my mother's corpse on the gurney,
she didn't see the sun that had seeped into nearly every pore
in those final years when my parents spent one month
each winter in Ft. Myers; she didn't see my mother beam
cherry pink at bingo games, at Perk-and-Glaze socials,
at water aerobics in the community pool where, each
morning, the women played a tape on a boom box
and drifted obligingly to the recorded instructions
but mostly used that hour to gossip about the women
who brought casseroles to widowed men who dotted the map
of the community like an epidemiological crisis. The nurse
couldn't have seen my mother's chest as broad and high as a shelf
as she floated in the shallow end of the pool; didn't see
my mother's fingers later that same day, fat as Vienna sausages,
offering Jay a little gray hot dog at the Red Sox spring training camp;
never saw my mother's toes as they squeezed
into the plastic sandals she insisted on buying at Kmart
in order to save money for the trips to Ft. Myers.
Attentive as she was to the donor sticker on my mother's
driver's license, the nurse didn't think *liver, kidney*; she certainly
didn't think *heart*. As she surveyed the body free of needle pricks,
surgical scars, amputations, bruises, and every other mark
of long-term illness, she thought *skin*, so easily flayed
from the body, a drape that, once released, could hang
on anyone, anywhere, perhaps in bits, perhaps in whole parts,
no longer *Queen Bee*, mother, wife, no longer
a tightened knot, aorta's squeeze, fallen chambers
of the heart, the stopped rush of blood in the veins.
Now just epidermis: expansive, generous, promiscuous,
so capable of protecting the body of another.

## What My Father Eats

Barely anything, but when he does feel a pang
      he opens the freezer and reaches for any one

of many meals my mother prepared and froze
      until the day she tumbled to the kitchen floor

and did not rise again. The orange-tinted arroz con pollo,
      dated September 1, straight from the Dragone

ricotta cheese container, scrubbed and re-used
      so many times that the graphic of the dragon

has almost vanished. The stuffed green peppers
      with ground beef, dated October 4, from the recycled

Cool Whip container. The caldo gallego from the
      Land O' Lakes margarine tub, the same caldo

that his mother taught my mother how to make
      right after they were married and right before

my grandmother was driven wild with her own pathetic
      maladies. He takes one meatball at a time

from the Dannon yogurt container, then drops it
      into the saucepan as he waits for the spaghetti

to boil and soften in a separate saucepan as per
      the directions on the Prince spaghetti box.

He eats the already-breaded-and-baked chicken
      even though, once defrosted, it's a little soggy,

even though he never cared for the way
      she did that, cooking and then freezing foods

that would have been much tastier when fresh, even though,
      once retired, she had the time to cook from scratch.

Whatever crystals have formed, no matter how long
    the food has been stored there, whatever mist

of halogenated hydrocarbons emanates
    from the freezer when he opens the door, it is always

a relief to the heat of his grieving, but perhaps even greater
    is the sight of her handwriting, there

on the tiny strips of white paper, Scotch-taped
    to each recycled container. The Palmer method

that she had learned from the nuns as a girl;
    the careful grip on the fountain pen's nib;

the pressure on the point after dipping, the strong
    connecting strokes, the body of each character,

the curved back of her majuscule *D*s, the strong head
    of one *O*, the small foot of another, the arms

of her *L*s and *T*s extending upward, the stubby legs
    of her small *N*s. In every ascender and descender

the rhythmic push-and-pull of each loop,
    the profound legibility of her hand.

## Cuba Libre

It's hard to know how or when an emotion turns
from its original liquid into the mineral hardness
of finished feeling. Last night at dinner, Gayle remembered

his fifth-grade project on the Armada, which allowed him
to light small boats on fire then sink them in the portable tub
his mother brought to school for the occasion; Jay recalled

his report on rubber, which taught him that the Mayans
dipped their feet into pools of rubber latex for fine-fitting shoes;
and Abram boasted of his fifth-grade research project on Cuba.

He loved how a tiny island nation that had been pimped out
to United Fruit and the casinos of Fulgencio Batista
finally refused to serve every carnal need of the United States.

It's hard now in the wake of Castro's botched belly operation
to imagine the force of that man, his ability to rock a whole
hemisphere, or a time when my father would be called

to Hanscom Air Force Base to stay on guard until the crisis
was done, and perhaps hardest to imagine the motives
of my parents, who, in 1976, would dress my toddler brother

as Fidel Castro for Halloween. But that's how it is: your father
can be a man who at one moment is ready for the Revolution,
who believes so deeply in Castro's radical social change

that his friends refer to him as *The Cuban Rocket*, and in another
can be capable of working in the windowless security
of the military-industrial complex for thirty-eight years.

He went on seemingly benign business trips to Texas
and Alabama and always returned with souvenir T-shirts for us,
but had he really gone to Houston and Huntsville?

Or did Hanscom have a stash of freshly tagged T-shirts in a cupboard
for those times when technicians went to Cuba for the weekend,
my dark-skinned father passing with his last name and Marxist leanings

for the embodiment of the Cuban dream? For years he brought us
to Hanscom for movie night with military brats and let us use the gym,
and we regularly enjoyed the annual picnics where a bright machine

would press our pennies into portraits of the iconic domed building
at MIT. But we would never know what happened in those
high-clearance rooms, on those forbidding Taino shores.

My father, so affectionate and expressive, always willing
to reveal the subtle emotional topography of his days, will not speak
of those secrets. Once, when we saw *The Good Shepherd*,

I gave my dad a nudge when the lights went up to say,
*Did that bring back some memories, ol' Pap? A reminder
of your shenanigans in Cuba?* and he didn't bite, just grinned

and changed the subject with *Where did we park, anyway?*
As we looked I wondered about that time in 1961.
On that cool dawn in October, my father left his new house,

knowing that by the end of the week, everything on the planet
would either emanate a deadly radiance or life would go on
as it had before—donut at breakfast, tuna at lunch, TV

at night, and eventually, children. Perhaps, then, it isn't such a leap
to imagine my parents, years later, as they dressed my little brother
as baby Castro, complete with greasepaint beard, the already-heavy

eyebrows of a brooding Spaniard, the olive green military uniform
and tiny plastic cigarillo. For the amusement of the guests
last night, I inserted the DVD with the hazy image and everyone

could see the easy irony: the simulated wood cupboards and table,
the seashell nightlight, the orange patterns on the no-wax linoleum,
and the weirdness of baby Castro traipsing through a neighborhood

during the height of the Cold War. In its brevity it was a perfect
post-dinner anecdote, but something in me felt shame for enjoying
the little boy who pushed me away onscreen and shook his fist at the camera,

saying, *No, no* in Super-8 silence to a parent who for all those years
dwelt in secrets and outrage for us, children who grow and leave
and leave again. It's enough to turn anyone to stone with grieving.

## Demeter's Last Stand

Last night, I alluded to my years as a Camp Fire Girl
and Averill revealed that she had been one, too,
and after she made the sign of a fire rising from her hand,

we chanted the promise that every Camp Fire Girl knows:
*WoHeLo means work; I light the candle of work. WoHeLo means*
*health; I light the candle of health. WoHeLo means love;*

*I light the candle of love.* How many times
did Lori Dembkoski and I giggle
during those camping expeditions in the backyard

of Mrs. D'Angelo, a kind woman who seemed to have invented
recycling when she filled her old knee-highs with soap chips
and knotted the ends to tree branches; when she poked

holes in gallon jugs and forced twigs into them
so that we could start and stop the water
as the jugs swung, unwieldy, from low branches;

when she told ghost stories that originated in her own house.
After a few years, Mrs. D'Angelo left us for a job
in Pennsylvania, and our new troop had to meet

in the low-ceilinged cafeteria at the middle school
where we resigned ourselves to cutting ochre-colored felt
amidst the stench of Tater Tots. I don't know how long

it took for a janitor named Connie Rock to find us,
but our encounters with him in the hallway
did offer surprises. One week he'd kneel down

to compliment our felt handiwork and knee-socks;
another time he'd ask us to sit on his lap just for a little while;
and eventually we kissed him on his sallow cheeks

that were soured and lined with decades of hard drink
and smoke. One night, when all the parents
came to the cafeteria for an event

not worth the remembering, Connie found me
and called my name, and I went to him as I had
in the weeks before. I imagine now what my mother

saw then: the red sash full of badges that she had hand-sewn,
the blue hat that featured a small bright bird;
my smile at an old janitor as he cradled me on his lap

and smiled back, as if I were Persephone and he were Hades,
just after he had pushed through a cleft in the soil to steal me.
It only took a moment for my mother to seize my wrist

and hurry to the car. Mother, if I thanked you too little,
know that tonight I remember your besting of Demeter's speed,
and that you saved me from a lifetime of winters.

TWO EMERGENCIES

*after Bruegel's Landscape with the Fall of Icarus*

These days, I don't see just the tiny legs
        of Icarus flailing
in the ice-cold waves, the plowman
        steering his obedient horse,
and the shepherd looking up to expose
        his face to the radiance of the sun.
I see the warhead that was stored
        in an unlocked potato shed
in a small Ukrainian town,
        I see it smuggled across the Caucasus
to Iran, I see it hitting the surface
        of the water in the nanosecond
before the nuclear holocaust.
        When I remember that it's not
a question of *if* but *when*,
        I can imagine everything
within the frame of that painting
        and that final explosion.
Today, in El Bruc, there's only one
        pharmacy, one grocery, a public
swimming pool, and a bar, and from here,
        I can hike all the way up
to the Black Virgin of Montserrat. I can eat
        salchichón and Manchego every day
as a merienda, and I can watch
        the grape leaves crackle and drift
from the trellis to the outdoor table
        as a man, at ten in the morning,
drinks his beer and listens
        to the car radio. Everyone's doing their best,
acting as if a bomb isn't
        about to detonate at any minute,

and some act as if bombs
        haven't detonated at all. Two days
after the Towers became ash,
        my mother bought me a toaster from Kmart
and asked about my wedding plans
        as she would have on any other day.
At the time, I thought *callous*, but now
        I think *constant*. I like to believe
that we have evolved because of figures
        like Icarus, but you don't have to be
an Old Master to know that isn't
        the whole story. That plowman?
Of course he heard the splash,
        the sounds of a drowning man. But he
had no idea how to swim, no interest
        in knowing, and you'd have to be
a goddamned idiot to abandon your horse
        and create two emergencies
where there was just one. Why not
        tend to your own horse. Why not
go home to a crappy toaster
        that sticks every time you push the lever.

# THE WATCH LIST

Is it too late to write about the watch list?
Still over one million names on the watch list.

Ted Kennedy, Mandela, and veterans with the residue
of gunpowder on their boots populate the watch list.

Twelve Robert Johnsons! Maybe one made a deal
with the devil. Guitar virtuosity bumps you up the watch list.

Saddam Hussein (after his death), the 9/11 hijackers
(also after death): my companions on the watch list.

When my father flies, he wears good trousers, cordovan
shoes for special occasions. He never travels watch-less.

The blood of Islam runs in every Spanish vein.
Perhaps that's why some of us are watched thus.

One of twenty methods of interrogation and vetting,
the most benign of which is the TSA watch list.

"To understand just one life, you have to swallow
the world." I believe you, Salman: you're on their watch list.

One man shackled to the chair as his wife waits
without food. Through plexiglass, she watches, listless.

"Oh yeah. In the new century, I think we will all
be insane." Diaz is halfway there. Watch this.

## Visit to Fox Hill Cemetery

Everywhere I look, the names of ghosts—
Cangiamila, Ciampi, DelMonico—
are freshly inscribed on stones that form a wreath
around my mother's. Ornate performances
of devotion: multicolored lighthouses,
huge tennis rackets, the faces of the dead etched
to match favorite photographs. To elaborate
upon their losses, mourners have left other
adornments: giant bouquets of flowers,
seashells from Hyannis, sashes from the Knights
of Columbus, all such frail laminates of joy.
I ask about the plant beside her stone
and Dad says, *Art Trepaney might have planted that.*
He takes the small, quickly wrapped bouquet
from under his arm and places it near the plant.
The clear plastic crinkles against the granite
and scatters the birds that peck among the headstones.

Days after her death, my mother didn't hide
in that place that was no place. She busily thrived
as the starling that stared at Nila all afternoon;
as the falcon that hovered above Alonso's boat;
as the sparrow that scratched the top of Jay's head
twice on his jog along the Lake Shore trail;
and once, as a kinglet, ruby-crowned, bobbing
and floating like a feisty pugilist at our front window.

If the dead can transform themselves into birds,
then why can't we become more like elephants?
When they bend
to their knees in the shade, they gently touch
the bodies of the dead, use their trunks

as pincers to lift and drape leaves of grass
across the body, then join in a circle
as if the dead might still be capable of finding comfort
in the sweetness of such profound keening. But no,
we are prisoners of our bodies. No metamorphosis
for living humans, not even for a little while.

RESILE

My mother's was a death
                without death.
        I didn't have to see it; she barely

had to endure it; and from the time
                of the phone call
        to the night of the wake, I could imagine

anything, or nothing. For my father,
                it was months
        of catastrophe. But me? I can return

to my original position
                after being stretched or compressed
        or bent. I can shrink, I can recoil,

I can repudiate. Like a strong
                synthetic material, I can absorb energy
        when subjected to strain, reach

my elastic limit, then seem
                the same as when you found me
        on the rack. Tonight, Peter

is a newly hooded doctor, and our friends
                dance beneath the ambient lights.
        At parties like this, I love

to corner people, and so too,
                it seems, does Peter's mother,
        a woman whom I have never met

before tonight, though I have known
                her son for years.
        The melancholy in her watery eyes

is her son's,
>	and whatever borders
>	once governed her body

have dissolved, or perhaps
>	were never there. Her empathy
>	is a wave of liquid matter, a tide

of fellow feeling. Three seasons have passed
>	and I haven't
>	had to feel anything, but this mother,

what does she do to me, listening so well
>	to my story
>	of sudden loss. Who is

this mother, so able to lift
>	her own grief to the surface:
>	the frail parents who vanished, slowly,

one at a time; the sons who love her best
>	but shout impatiently
>	on the phone; the self-help books she reads

so that she can better love her husband.
>	Why, when we speak
>	of my mother's death, does her empathy

break the synthetic bonds in me,
>	so that when
>	I try to reconstitute myself, I see

that she is holding my hand, water
>	holding water,
>	and that this won't stop for some time.

In my father's favorite photo,

she's eight years old and has just received
first Eucharist. The dress, veil, and even
the tiny white prayer book have been borrowed
from a cousin in Revere. She stares
beyond the lens with a look that predates
the night she met him in a house
that is no longer a house on Maverick Street,
before she entered the church
that was renovated into condos
once the rats left, before she realized
that the world is full of change, and that life
is merely opinion. To my father's relief,
she was born with these suspicions, born
to doubt. When, at Easter, he shows the picture
to Dora and Dee, they laugh out loud.
They know that look, and now, after
the deep grooves of grief, they can enjoy
the black-and-white stasis, the gelatin
and linen rags that keep her in one place.

## EMERSON IN MOURNING

In these early weeks of November, my mother's spirit
             still wanders like a planet, but her body
       is hard and heavy as a potato, an onion, a rock

buried deep enough to forbid the casual excavation.
             I know he has considered it, and except for us,
       he would do it. The day before she died, he read

about how, when Emerson was a young man,
             his wife died of tuberculosis. The tall, shy minister
       would walk from downtown Boston to Roxbury

every day to visit her grave. One day, after many
             during which he could not bear the loss,
       Emerson opened his wife's coffin. I know

that my father's final look was not enough.
             Even worse, every feature seemed wrong:
       the bloated face that was more Albert Finney

than Queen Bee; the rosary beads wrapped around
             her fingers; the enormous crucifix above her head.
       Perhaps he thinks, as I do, that the corpse belonged

to someone else, not my mother, who had once
             said, *I'm too mean to die.* No, he won't dig
       the soil and open the casket. My father is no Emerson.

Rather, he will go to the back room of our split ranch
             and weep without consolation.
       I will listen to him through the porch door

and see the windows opening out to the snow
             all around, the quiet of the basketball court
       that we haven't used in years, the picnic table covered

with a faded tarp. He will moan a long, loud dirge,
             and it will be hard to know if it's meant
       to push her to oblivion or bring her back.

## A Billerica Romance

When I told Peter that my parents did not have a Hollywood romance,
      he, with his usual Whitmanesque expansiveness, said, *Jo. Of course*

*not. They had a Billerica romance*, putting the oxymoron together
      as if it were a tautology. His conviction made it seem possible

that Billerica could be a Wuthering Heights, a Casablanca,
      a Paris, some fantasy place where four years of double-dating

could be enough to know someone, a place where, when your girlfriend
      asks you to take her to see Doris Day in *Calamity Jane* and Deborah Kerr

in *Tea and Sympathy* and Beryl Reid in *The Killing of Sister George*
      so that she can see "how the other half lives," you don't stop

to think that it's unusual, even after her years of education
      in all-girl schools. At Fitton, she loved those nuns who never

really taught her to ask *how* or *why*, unless it was *How well do you stitch*
      *white thread on black cloth?* and *How much Horace can you memorize*

*in the original Latin?* So you don't ask *how* or *why* either, because the name
      for that kind of love is only a few decades old, and even then

barely visible to the average man. You date, you marry, and she
      approaches romance, or at least a story about it. And when

she invites her women friends from the telephone company
      for a Christmas-in-July party, you don't mind that it's an all-girl thing,

a chance to swap Christmas decorations, bake favorite cookies, wear
      the fuzzy red hats, and play the Johnny Mathis LP, a record

that was simply too sweet for just a few weeks between Thanksgiving
      and Epiphany. In every way, those parties were better than real Christmas:

no children or husbands to spoil the pure pleasure
      of too-sloppy icing and naughty stocking stuffers, no loneliness

for those women who never married or had children
in the first place, who willingly worked

on Christmas, day and night, for years until their quiet retirements.
And later, after the children and the routines of domesticity,

you never begrudged her the pleasures of DVDs and streaming videos
of *The "L" Word*, her favorite show in those last months, especially

since her favorite friendship had withered so painfully. Without
a call, without an explanation, the friendship vanished as easily

and inexplicably as an image from the screen. In one of our last phone calls
she said, *I miss Natalie so much. I think of her all the time*, in a plaintive voice,

a shocking admission from the toughest woman I've ever known.
There is a word for this, but no word for our inability to say it.

No, we will never say it or suggest it, even if we all know it, because this was,
after all, a Billerica romance, the most ordinary romance in the world.

# 3

## METASTASIS

## PRIDE AND PREJUDICE

Reader, if someday the heiress of a major American department store
calls and asks you to lead a discussion of *Pride and Prejudice*,

just remember that it is never a good idea to accept the invitation
if you harbor suspicions of the wealthy that could sully the discussion

of what is otherwise one of the most perfect novels ever written.
And if you do decide to take the job, don't, in the midst

of a conversation about the finances of Darcy and the Bennetts,
remind the women that their own worth is just as easy to find

on Google as the newest YouTube clip; don't listen to the women
begrudge the importance of money as they sip their tea; and don't

be surprised when they offer you no food and you find yourself
swooning, partly from midmorning hypoglycemia, partly

from the thought of what your mother laid out for the measliest
of events, your mother in her modest kitchen of linoleum

and Formica and petaled wallpaper and the overhead light
that turned even the cannolis a little blue. Above all,

don't be too disappointed when, after all the lively talk of women
"marrying up" and the urgent debate over why Jane Austen

is still a classic, the check that you receive for your services
is just big enough to buy a box of plastic ornaments

at the major American department store owned by the woman
who called you in the first place. Because, in the end, you are merely

an ornament, a bell tinkling on the giant tree of capitalism.
Remember this when, after seeing the amount on your check

and walking down the driveway full of Mercedes, you realize
that you have to use the toilet after all, and that when you knock

on the glass and they squint as if they have never seen you before,
it is because they see a strand of tinsel, a silvery nothing, waiting to drift back in.

TAKE UP AND READ

When Augustine sat beneath the fig tree
and announced the lines that led to his conversion,
    his friend Alypius was so moved

    that he too read aloud from the Bible
and in doing so revised his life. Thank goodness
    those noisy days are over, because

    if Lori Dembkoski and I had read aloud
from the book we found in my parents' basement
    during one of her sleepovers,

    we would have appalled even ourselves,
though perhaps Augustine might have shown an interest
    during his younger, lustier years

    when he prayed, *Lord, make me pure, but not yet.*
The book's mustard-yellow cover announced,
    *Everything You Always Wanted*

    *to Know about Sex\* (\*but were afraid to ask)*
and was loosely traced with webs and dots of dead mites,
    which said something

    about either our housekeeping habits
or my parents' practical approach to having sex
    in the '70s. Late at night, Lori and I

    would scan the question-answer format
of the book that, in its 27th printing, was *the incredible phenomenon*
    *that started a "sex" manual revolution!*

    We couldn't help but believe in a book
that relied on the research of Drs. Kwint, Schlom,
    and Cranny. If they said that eunuchs

grow up to be tall, pale, thin, and mean,
then how could we disagree, especially when most boys
        in the fifth grade seemed to fit

        that description? And what a relief
it was to know that a penis can't really disappear, except
        in the mind of its owner;

        that transvestites rarely enjoy
wearing capris or ladies' stretch pants; and that a husband
        really likes a sexy massage

        after a tough day with the boss.
I wondered: did our neighbors know
        that Spanish fly is an extract

        derived from the green blister beetle
of southern Europe, and that rat poison can be
        a powerful aphrodisiac, unless,

        of course, it kills you? As we leafed
through the yellowing pages, I imagined the Bellonis,
        the Rossinis, the Baldassaris, and my parents

        all receiving a complimentary copy
of the book with the final sale of each new house
        in the development, part of the dream

        of identical windows and lawns
and doors and beams of lumber that still
        smelled freshly cut. One night,

        after we were alternately baffled
then impressed by the section on shoe fetishes,
        Lori and I tiptoed upstairs

        to steal slices of American cheese
from the refrigerator. Lori unpeeled her slice
        then flung it up, whole, to the ceiling,

where it lodged in the swirled stucco.
As the years passed, the slice turned brown, then gray,
and eventually Lori performed her own conversion

in the backseat of a school bus, on a band trip
to Norwalk, Connecticut. She returned like Walter Raleigh
with stories of a foreign land of heavy petting,

while I had stayed behind, practicing
my clarinet in the basement, occasionally taking breaks
to read about Arnold, a stockbroker

who wore a mirror on his shoe to see
the "entire situation" under a librarian's dress;
and Gene, who thankfully extricated

his penis from the eager jaws
of his girlfriend's surprisingly tight vagina. Later,
when my parents were convinced

that the stuccoed cheese was a leak
that required fixing, I didn't confess,
though my mind remained fixed in those pages.

## Metastasis, Boracay

When we travel, I'm usually so drunk on a cocktail
of panic mixed with boredom, so busy calculating
the peso-to-dollar conversion, so certain that I'll contract

the dengue fever from the one stubborn mosquito
that'll penetrate the sheer bedroom netting
that I forget how much beauty each new thing possesses

and how some beauty requires an initial sickness,
an irritation, often in the form of a foreign body.
In the case of pearls, the sickness—

a burr in an otherwise milky trance of protein—
happens too infrequently. Centuries ago, the Philippines
were full of divers: scores of slaves pushed overboard

to plunge deep for the baroque imperfection of small,
radiant knobs hiding among the sharks and poisonous
jellyfish. I remembered this as I dipped underwater

in my snorkel mask and fins, then rose above again
to see Jay's mother and aunts onshore, hunched beside
a young man whose suitcase was full of pearls—pink,

smoky gray, bright white—fake pearls that cost pennies
in American money. How could something so beautiful
cause no pain, no harm, and bring such delight

to three thrifty women on vacation in Boracay,
an island that seemed more like a Hollywood movie set
than a real place? I dipped below again to see the pinkish tips

of a coral reef that took thousands of years to form
now being grazed by the foot of Uncle Ming, too tall
for the ascending filigree, his eyes still dimly lit

from the bottles of San Miguel that rattled
in the back seat of the van, his red swimsuit billowing
and swollen, almost alive in the clear water. The coral,

once touched, turned instantly to dust, a millennial cloud
lifting in the filtered light. I pushed back to the surface
to ask the boatsman if this was right—the shallow waters,

the high reef—but I didn't. Uncle Ming took another swig,
laughed freely with his brother and nephew,
and looked up to dry his face in the hot sun.

Later, he lay on the white sand to make an angel
with his swooping arms and legs, indulged in a plate
of crawfish heaped on rice as if he were the king

of Boracay. Even then it must have been growing
in him: the nacreous luster swelling his lungs,
its concretion an opalescence that would drift

to the brain, spine, and liver. Just like *metastasis*,
a flitting of words from one idea to the next,
a fish waving its fins through the coral's last rise.

## Uncle Ming Pinched Me

While some cousins confirmed the funeral arrangements
and others browsed sales racks for the right thing to wear,

we sat at the table with little else to do but eat,
and just as I was about to put a succulent piece

of *adobo* into my mouth, Cousin Jeannie said,
*In his final hour I felt him pinch me*, and of course

I thought what anyone would if they had known Ming
when he was well: Good work, you sly fox! Sick as a dog

with chemicals indiscriminately fighting every cell
of your body, and still you had the moxie

of a true rascal. For a moment I imagined
the long list of women he might have goosed in his life:

big ones, skinny ones, young ones who didn't know
how to fry eggs the morning after, all lining up

to greet him as he entered the pearly gates.
But what Jeannie really meant was this:

that as the last trickles and swirls of whiskey and smoke
vanished from his bloodstream; as his body finally

bloated then withered into a spent balloon;
and as the spirit that made him the single agnostic

among his devoted family faded unremarkably
into a wash of gray, Cousin Jeannie felt a light pinch

on her forearm, just as she was putting her youngest
child to sleep. Later, after coffee, Auntie Jessie

recalled the text message she received on her cell phone
before Ming died, which read: *Please say a special prayer*

*for Ming today*, a message from an unknown number,
which led everyone at the table to believe

that it was God who sent it, or if not God
then perhaps some other force that knew Ming

needed an extra boost, *especially* Ming, who, as Uncle Jun
noted, was the philosopher of the family, the one

who walked out of the healing Mass when he thought
it was a bunch of baloney, all that flailing and whooping

and fainting, which, years earlier, had once sent Uncle Jun
into a swoon so profound that Auntie Jessie raced to catch him

from behind, and in doing so collapsed from the weight
and cracked two of her ribs. But why change Ming in death,

when in life he was remarkable, above all, for his consistent
and honest observations of this world? When I last saw him healthy,

it was in the Philippines, when we traveled together
for weeks in crowded vans on congested roads.

Through the van's tinted windows, we saw so many
gigantic billboards for skin lightening creams

and chemicals that transformed wavy hair
into a waxy sheen that I had to ask about them,

and he said, *Don't you understand that Filipinas want
to be white? They want to look like you, smell like you, be you.*

And in that moment race seemed like a disease
with a simple outline, a form that could be quickly drawn,

just like the pencil sketch that Albrecht Dürer
created for his doctor friend, a picture of himself

unclothed, pointing to his abdomen with an inscription
that read: *This is where I hurt.* Amid the screech of roosters

and the clouds of smog that permeated
the neighborhoods of Manila, Ming's voice

was not a pinch or a float, a falling toward life
or a rising from the dead, but a bell sounding

against self-delusion. There was some small shard
of iron left in his irony, a place where suffering didn't entirely

break. But that was just one part of his negotiation
with God, of the drawing that pointed to the pain.

## My Funny Valentine

Nearly done now with this winter of grieving
        and everywhere I see a wing, a flourish,
    a flower emerging from the pupa

of February's closet. I sit at the reception
        for Art and Sue, septuagenarian widowers
    who, only months ago, fell in love

while walking their dogs, and this afternoon vowed
        *I do* until the end of their days.
    On every plate, a small origami triangle

springs alive: dozens of multi-colored cranes
        folded by the deacon of the Tewksbury
    Congregationalist Church. Between the green salad

and the fruit cocktail, a woman named Serena
        tells me that she is a nurse practitioner,
    and Paul—perhaps her partner, perhaps

her friend—is an illustrator at Raytheon,
        but once he hears what my profession is,
    he tells me his real passion: dressing up

as Leonardo da Vinci and visiting classrooms
        to perform that man's genius.
    During the main course of roasted chicken,

we speak of Francis Bacon and his essays on marriage,
        how easily he borrowed from Montaigne
    to suggest that a friendship between men

was more valuable than any marriage
        with a woman; we speak of cross-dressing
    on Shakespeare's stage, the similarities

between a soft-faced boy and a full-grown woman.
How flexible the gender that bends
like an origami wing, like Paul

when he asks me to dance to the music
provided by my cousin, whose tribute to Elvis
has the whole joint grooving to every song.

An immodest dance, a little too close, during which
Paul asks, *Do you know something about me?*
Above the din of Robbie's final strains

of "An American Trilogy," Paul answers my puzzled look.
*I'm transgendered. By this time next month, I'll be Renee.*
*If you run your hand down my back you'll feel my bra.* No need;

I already feel the breasts, large and matronly.
They have already taken me back to the morning
my mother taught me the fox trot and box step

in our living room, she dancing the man's part,
the closest she would come
to her own transformation.

## In Praise of Silence

Amid the bump and boom of car stereos and the peal
of police car sirens, the monastery is a square of quiet
in this prairie city. When Brother Ignatius releases
the lock to let us in, we can barely hear the drift
of Gregorian chant in the chapel. We've come here
to write and read without interruption, and it mostly works:
the quiet of these devoted brothers ripples through each room,
the only interruption the occasional footfall
of Brother Ezekiel as he leaves our breakfast on a tray
at the bottom of the steps. I should learn something
from these Benedictines whose great ancestor lived
as a hermit in a cave with secrets of his own. Instead,
I am forensic in my every investigation; in this
and more, I am my mother's daughter. During one
of our writing breaks, I tell Laura what I know
about the night my mother lost every quality
of personhood: first, her thoughts as she surrendered
to her body's discomforts of indigestion then diarrhea,
then nausea and sweat; then the awareness of every detail,
which for her was both sword and shield in a war
no one else wanted to fight; then her language, always
sour as a lemon, until she lay, infant-like, on the bed without a word;
then memory itself, appearing as it did in frames
of black-and-white photos and hazy home videos.
This only a few weeks after my father had pointed
to where he had found my mother's body, one foot
caught under the bureau, face down on the floor. His eyes
looked into mine until he almost saw her again, and in his look
of sheer terror, it seemed possible that she was still present
and capable of exacting her revenge for those last hours.
At some point in my telling, the words become material things,
as when the angels come to deliver a message
in a Renaissance painting. They travel from my mouth
into Laura's body and she sways and leans against the wall

until she nearly loses consciousness, so great is the force
of my mother, still so close to us in those first weeks,
still so capable of punishing. But that's
another story, and there's no need to tell every story,
no need to tell everything I know.

## On the Meeting of Larry David and Antonin Artaud

after Philip Levine

In my dream, Antonin Artaud is a patient
at Bellevue, receiving electroshock treatments
for the schizophrenia that shattered him
for all of his adult life, and Larry David
has come to see him during visiting hours.
Antonin's eyes reveal a man who on most days
is frantic beyond reason, but today, Larry's
the one who's at the end of his rope.
He's just starred in his first feature-length film
and it's a flop. He knows he should never
have taken a role written thirty-five years ago
and intended for Zero Mostel, that great
heaving sweat machine who died too soon
to play the part. Larry's a writer, a comedian,
but no actor, and now he's stinking up
an already terrible movie. Even worse,
Larry's wife has left him—not just
in the TV show, but in real life too, and all
because he probably complained too much
about the environmentally sound toilet paper.

At first, it might seem unlikely that Larry
should meet this great French surrealist.
But Antonin had a soul that could find *the meaning
and fulfillment of its perfection only in its own disaster*,
and in this regard, he and Larry are twins
born of the same seed. So when Antonin
sees Larry insult a nurse, trip on the foot
of a demented patient, and swear out loud
three times as he crosses the floor of the ward,
Antonin feels delight, perhaps for the first time
in years. Finally, a man who might slice
the veneer of bourgeois reality in two!

Larry is also having a good time. Blind
to socioeconomic distinctions, oblivious
to mental illness or wellness, Larry is pleased
with Antonin's frenetically spun moustache
and pulls on it in the hope that it's a fake.

In a few minutes, visiting hours will end,
and Larry will return to the lonely world
outside, the one that Antonin abandoned
years ago. The men look out the window,
first to the East River and the barges floating
downstream, and then, beyond the water
to the length of Long Island City, the old
PepsiCo sign a halo of bright red curves.
To Antonin, the sign is an interminable Rorschach test,
the answers to which he will never know.
To Larry, it is a reminder that he is thirsty.
When he goes to the vending machine
he loses his change after he pushes the button.
He walks away in disgust, and just as he
is about to leave the ward, he hears
the rubbery footfall of the nurse
whom he had insulted only minutes earlier.
She pushes the same button and gets two Pepsis,
but will not give one to Larry, who takes out
his small notebook to resume his endless work.

## THE APPALACHIAN ITALIAN AMERICANS

In one photo, Uncle Joe stands as stiff and opaque
  as marble. He holds two bronze bells, but by the way
he's lowered them to his sides, you can tell
  he has no intention of ringing them. Beside him,
Auntie Michelina waves a brave American flag
  and leans against a giant panda that Cousin Jerry
must have won the night before at the local carnival.
  In front of Michelina, little Eddie wears a dress shirt
and gym shorts with dark socks and dress shoes.
  This ten-year-old boy will one day grow up to run
for office, and as a souvenir will print his name
  on every plastic comb in the county, but for now,
he is belting out his best tambourine routine,
  and, with legs apart, seems as if he is just about to leap
into a military march, while behind him, his sister
  holds the pink carnations that are a welcome gift to my mother
and father. You see, this is a kind of receiving line.
  My parents are newlyweds, and they have just taken
a few days off to drive from Boston to Uniontown
  to meet this side of the family, the tomato-growing,
grapevine-loving, square-dance-hopping, Pittsburghese-
  twanging, Afro-sporting, coal-mining, church-going
Appalachian Italian Americans. As if in disbelief,
  my father hides his face from the camera,
and my mother reaches out to receive the carnations
  from her cousin. From the way she reaches with both hands,
she might be clapping, or she might be wondering where
  to put them next, or she might be focused on something
beyond the asbestos-sided houses and auto-body repair shop
  and the land that rises, bubbles, and faults for hundreds of miles
in every direction. *There's something beyond this*, her look
  seems to say. *Surely there's something beyond this.*

# Notes

"Larry David on Corregidor": Corregidor is an island about twenty miles west of Manila. "Corregidor" is most likely derived from the Spanish *corregir*—to correct. The island was used as a fortress and a prison during the era of Spanish colonization, and then as a base for American and Filipino troops during World War II.

"Pyrrhic": This poem draws its materials from the etchings on an ancient Greek oil jar at the Art Institute of Chicago and from the phrase "Art can make war look wrong" from Stephen Burt's review of Bruce Smith's *Devotions* in the *New York Times Book Review* from August 7, 2011.

"77 Porter Street": The final lines of this poem are inspired by Elaine Scarry's *The Body in Pain*.

"The anatomy of my melancholy": This poem is inspired by Robert Burton's *Anatomy of Melancholy*.

"Thank You, Brian Williams": "the purple testament of bleeding war" is a quote from Shakespeare's *Richard II*.

"Erasure": This is an erasure of Michel de Montaigne's essay "Of Sadness."

"The Watch List": The first quote is the epigraph from Salman Rushdie's *Midnight's Children*. The second quote comes from Tony Kushner's *Angels in America: Millennium Approaches*.

"On the Meeting of Larry David and Antonin Artaud": The italicized quote comes from an essay by Maurice Saillet in Artaud's book titled *The Theater and Its Double*. The inspiration for this poem comes from a *New Yorker* "Talk of the Town" article that reported that psychiatrists were showing schizophrenic patients episodes of *Curb Your Enthusiasm* as part of a new therapy.